THE FISH WE CATCH

By the same author (Fully bound books)

PAPERFRONTS

THE FISH WE CATCH

IDENTIFICATION — HABITAT — LURES

Written and Illustrated
By W. E. DAVIES

PAPERFRONTS

ELLIOT RIGHT WAY BOOKS

KINGSWOOD, SURREY, U.K.

This is a Crown Octavo Book
set in eleven point "Monotype" Times

*Made and Printed in Great Britain by
Cox and Wyman, Ltd., London, Reading and Fakenham*

For
Alfred, Sylvia,
and Marion

ACKNOWLEDGEMENT

I desire here to thank the Editors of the following magazines for permission to use quotations from articles of mine that have appeared in *Fishing Gazette*, *Trout and Salmon*, *Shooting Times*, *Midland Angler*, and *Stream and Field in Ireland*.

W. E. DAVIES

CONTENTS

Contents

Part III

SALTWATER FISH

INTRODUCTION

MY idea in writing this book is to tell in as few words as possible how to identify the catch; the habitat of the fish being sought and the best methods to use in their capture.

To this end baits and tackles are illustrated with the species concerned.

To make for easy reference the book is divided into three parts: Game Fish, Freshwater Fish (I detest the words "coarse fish"), and Saltwater Fish.

I have dealt with forty species which I think represents the major portion of the kinds of fish we anglers—excluding specialists—catch. Granted there are others, but to deal with them all would entail a much bigger work than this.

Moving about these isles, wetting a line here and there, I have more than once been amazed at the lack of knowledge exhibited on the fascinating subject of fish identification. Another thing that has always interested me is the many names some fish have. Within the distance of a few miles some species have their names changed two or three times. Wherever possible local names are included.

Methods of capture, tackle and baits to be used, will always form the basis of argument wherever anglers meet. Rightly so, because each and every one of us has

11

a pet idea on how this or that should be done. In that facet of the sport lies most of the charm and appeal of angling.

However, I say this, when fish are uncooperative the wise angler experiments and so new methods are born. But, the *modus operandi* given in respect of each fish dealt with in the following pages are the ones that have stood the test of time.

PART I

GAME FISH

Bull Trout
Common Trout
Char
Grayling
Lake Trout

Loch Leven Trout
Rainbow Trout
Salmon
Sea Trout

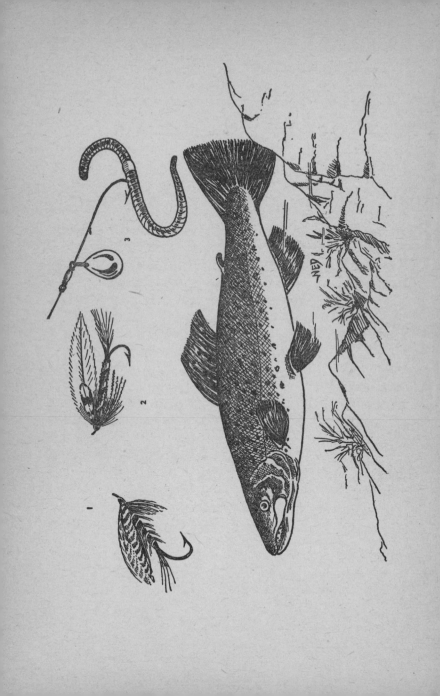

BULL TROUT

Local Names: **Round-tail, Bully, Mock Salmon**

How to Identify

Powerful, rounded tail, body olive-bronze, belly a dirty white, jaws studded with sharp teeth. The whole fish is covered with big black and brown spots and has the outward appearance of a large brown trout. The flesh is flabby and a dirty whitish-yellow in colour, it is not such good eating as a brown trout and is very inferior to salmon or sea trout. A grand fighter it prefers to battle it out with long runs, but rarely takes to the air.

Habitat

Prefers deep, rocky pools in which it lies dormant during day-time coming out to feed on minnows, etc., as soon as the light begins to fade. It is a menace to salmon as it chases them off the spawning beds. This trait in its make-up is believed to be the reason for it being called bull trout. In Northumberland it is always referred to as the "bully", in Scotland it is often called round-tail or mock salmon. There are very few salmon

Illustration Key
1. Salmon fly
2. Streamer fly
3. Worm with spoon

rivers that do not have a bull trout or two during the season.

How to Catch

The bull trout is not fussy and will strike at most baits, being particularly obliging in this respect during late summer and early autumn.

A good bait to use in a pool known to hold a few "bullies" is a large lobworm worked in conjunction with a spoon.

For spinning baits a blue and silver devon or the same size in brown and gold are good after a flood when the water is about to clear.

At night "swimming" a bunch of worms down into a pool is a good method and a few years ago while fishing the Tweed I saw a 16-lb. bull trout caught in this way. The biggest runs of this ocean-loving trout occur in the River Tweed and its tributaries and the River Coquet (Northumberland).

Rods and tackle should be the same as those used when after salmon.

COMMON TROUT

How to Identify

In many localities trout vary in colour due to their environment. For instance I have caught trout from Dartmoor streams that have been almost black and from the Coquet in Northumberland I have taken fish with a golden-yellow coloration. However, the general characteristics are the same. Small head, large eyes, thick wrist to the tail which is forked and the dorsal fin is more fleshy at the base and looks much stronger than that of its brother, the Loch Leven trout. It is the most widely distributed of all the trouts and one of the most game.

Habitat

Trout like humans have to eat to live and the places that provide the most food will produce the best fish. Wherever there is fresh and pure water coming into the main flow there trout will be found to congregate. Instinct tells them that such places, being healthy, produce the best food insects of all kinds. However, if such a spot is minus reasonable cover, good fish will only feed there in the late evening and under cover of darkness. Isolated weed beds well out from the bank are a sure sign of spring water bubbling up. Such beds are meal-tables to trout for all kinds of insects breed there. Under-cut banks, at the sides of large sunken boulders and tree roots and trunks are all possible haunts for good fish. The 6- and

7-in. trout will "sport" in the streamy water in their chase for insects but the big fellows like their food to come to them and so they lie and wait for the water to bring it to them. What is more, my experience has taught me that the larger a trout gets the more lazy he becomes, so take your time when fishing the spots mentioned.

How to Catch

At the commencement of a season nymphs and wet flies are best, but as the temperature rises and insects begin hatching the dry fly can be used. However, it has been my experience that the wet fly will usually take the heaviest fish. In mid summer when the streams are low and clear, providing your licence permits it, reasonable sport can be had by using natural bait such as caterpillars, beetles, craneflies (daddy-longlegs), maggots, etc.

In river fishing the hook sizes range from 12 to 18 and in lakes, including reservoirs, 10 to 14. A gut cast is best for wet fly-fishing as it sinks more readily and for dry fly, nylon will be found to assist in keeping the fly afloat as it is much more buoyant than silkworm gut.

In conclusion it is interesting to note that the trout that are now so plentiful in New Zealand are the offspring of trout from England. A consignment of trout eggs was sent there by Frank Buckland in January 1864. These eggs were taken from fish that had been netted from a tributary of the River Itchen, at Bishopstoke, near Winchester.

Illustration Key

1. Caterpillar (natural)
2. Cranefly (natural)
3. Mayfly
4. Wet fly
5. Nymph
6. Dry fly

CHAR

In all families at some time or another an aristocrat makes an appearance and the Salmonidæ is no exception for with the char we have the most colourful member. It is not so widely distributed as trout and it does not grow to a great size. In England the only worth-while place to fish for them is Lake Windermere. In North Wales there are a few mountain lakes holding a species of char and in Scotland and Ireland there are a number of lakes which hold them.

The sketch is that of a Welsh char (Torgoch) a few of which are caught each year from the deep-water lakes near Snowdon.

During my fifty years fishing I have caught about thirty char not one of which has been over a pound weight. All have been brightly coloured the predominating hue being red.

Habitat

It loves deep, cold water and only enters the feeder streams to spawn when they can then be taken on brightly coloured flies.

Illustration Key
1. Plumb-line bait as used on Lake Windermere
2. Small salmon fly

How to Catch

With the exception of the Lake District where they are fished for with deeply-worked plumb lines the char is occasionally taken by anglers when trolling a gold devon for lake trout. The char bait of Windermere is not rounded like a devon but is flat and spins and wobbles like a spoon. It is invariably coloured gold and is made to work within a few inches of the lake bottom.

At one time so prolific were the char in Windermere that an industry was set up there for "potting" char. The fish are still there although not in such great numbers. But should you be deep trolling on a lake and catch a brilliant-coloured fish shaped like a trout, then you will have something to talk about for it will be a char.

On Windermere's feeder streams the Brathay and Rothay, late autumn usually marks the spawning run of char. Flies to use dressed on No. 8 or 10 hooks include the following salmon-fly patterns: Silver Wilkinson, Jock Scot, Silver Doctor, Durham Ranger, Fiery Brown and Black Goldfinch.

GRAYLING

Local Names: **Umber, Gray Lady, Lady of the Stream, Silver Lady**

THE grayling is a most convenient and obliging fish—the fly-fisher's stop-gap—coming into season as the trout go out and contrariwise. Broadly speaking, she (one always refers to this fish as she) stoops to conquer, and to be conquered, from Michaelmas to Candlemas, and lucky indeed is the angler who resides near grayling water for then he can carry on with his fly-fishing the whole year through.

It is not so widely distributed as the common trout; this is no doubt due to the fact that it requires a fairly high oxygen content in the water for it to thrive.

Two characteristics of the grayling are its colouring and the large dorsal fin. It is much faster of movement than a trout and in some parts of the north is called "Umber" to denote that it is like a grey shadow.

It is mainly an insect-diet fish and there are few records of it having taken live minnows as bait or artificial minnows.

Due to its large dorsal fin and silver and grey colouring it is easy to identify.

Habitat

Gravelly streams and pools are the most likely places

to look for grayling, but their haunts vary with the seasons. In the summer you will find them feeding in holes just below very fast water, but in the autumn they resort chiefly to the intervening shallows, loving especially the edge of the current. Later in the season they lurk in the placid depths and at the edge of frost-bitten weed beds.

How to Catch

During early autumn the dry fly will usually take a customer or two. In coloured water a cast of two wet flies will attract a brace or two, but always bear in mind when using flies that the best patterns for this species always have a little red in the dressing.

In winter when the Gray Lady is in tip-top condition both for sport and table, float fishing with maggots or a small red worm will invariably produce the best sport. However, on occasions, even natural baits will fail to charm her ladyship and then is the time to try the grasshopper. This is an artificial which bears little or no resemblance to the natural insect. In all grayling fishing err on the side of small hooks. For flies 14 and 16s are best and for maggot and worm 12 and 14s. The best type of grasshopper lures are those dressed on No. 10 or 12 hooks. Good fly patterns include: Red Tag, Iron Blue Dun, Bradshaw, Red Spinner and Red Palmer.

Illustration Key

1. Winged wet fly	4. Winged dry fly
2. Maggots	5. Worm
3. Spider wet fly	6. Grasshopper lure

LAKE TROUT

An ambition I have had for many years is to catch a 20-lb. trout. My lines have been wet in Canada, the U.S.A., Norway, and Finland, and the most likely places in the British Isles, but so far that particular sized trout has eluded me. Yet I know that in some of the lakes of Scotland and Ireland there lurk such monsters as a glance at the record book shows. The largest lake trout on record is a fish of $39\frac{1}{8}$ lb. from Loch Awe. Its nearest rival came from Lough Derg a mere $30\frac{1}{2}$ lb. in 1861, five years before the Loch Awe beauty. Since then we have had about eight lake trout of 20 lb. and over.

Habitat

Deep-water lakes that have plenty of natural food.

How to Catch

In Scotland and Ireland local anglers troll for them with natural bait (with spinning vanes attached) or long-shanked streamer flies and salmon flies. Where the haunt of a large trout is known the small group of anglers

Illustration Key

1. Minnow
2. Small salmon fly
3. Streamer fly
4. Worm
5. Silver devon

who know the location anchor a boat and fish with worms, live minnows, and young trout.

In Canada and the U.S.A. where I have seen a number of 20-lb. trout taken from the Big Lakes area the lines have always been of metal to withstand the pressure. Over there the fish is known as Gray Trout due to its coloration which is a combination of greys. Natural bait and large spoons are used as bait, on the troll.

However, in the British Isles the man who has set his mind on a 20-pounder can do no better than troll in those areas likely to support a fish of such dimensions.

Here are the names of a few waters known to hold monster trout: *Scotland:* Loch Awe, Loch Stennes, Loch Rannock. *Ireland:* Lough Ennel, Lough Derg, Lough Corrib.

LOCH LEVEN TROUT

Local Names: **Silver Trout, Silversides, The Scotsman's Trout**

How to Identify

Colorations in trout are many and varied. The Loch Leven trout is an example, with its silvery sides. The tail is more forked than the common trout although science is definite that it is an off-shoot. It is also more slim in build with not such powerful shoulders, and the spots— black, brown and sometimes bright vermilion—are not so pronounced as in the common trout.

Habitat

Until this century the Loch Leven trout was looked upon as essentially a lake fish. Angling became more popular with the turn of the century and Loch Leven fish were used to restock depleted streams. They flourished for the most part and are now distributed all over the world where water conditions suit them. A characteristic of this charming fish is that its flesh is a delightful pinkish colour and has a finer flavour than that of its brother.

In lakes, including reservoirs, it much prefers the shallow areas to those of deep water. On Loch Leven from where it originated the best and heaviest baskets have usually come from that section known as "The Shallows". In rivers and streams it likes streamy water providing it is not too fast or turbulent.

29

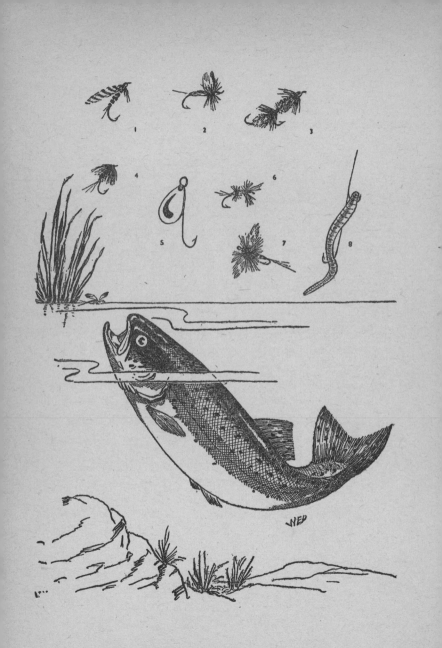

How to Catch

I think that the composer of that delightful little song "The Trout" must have had in mind a fish similar in form and characteristics to the Loch Leven while writing, for it is a most frolicsome fish. While it can be taken on artificial baits such as spoons and natural baits like worms and insects it is essentially a fly-fisherman's fish.

In the spring nymphs can be calculated to prove the undoing of a brace or two and as the water settles down the wet fly will come into its own, indeed such patterns can be used throughout the whole season. When the water temperature rises and flies start hatching with greater frequency, then the angler who can use the dry fly will invariably be assured of a tenant or two for his fern or grass-lined basket.

The Loch Leven trout is more active during the hours of daylight whereas the exact opposite is the case with the common trout,

Hook sizes for flies should range from No. 14 to 16, and flies include Greenwell's Glory, Wickham's Fancy, Peter Ross, March Brown, Iron Blue Dun and Teal and Red.

Illustration Key

1. Wet fly
2. Winged dry fly
3. Worm fly
4. Wet spider fly
5. Fly spoon
6. Nymph
7. Spent dry fly
8. Upstream worm tackle

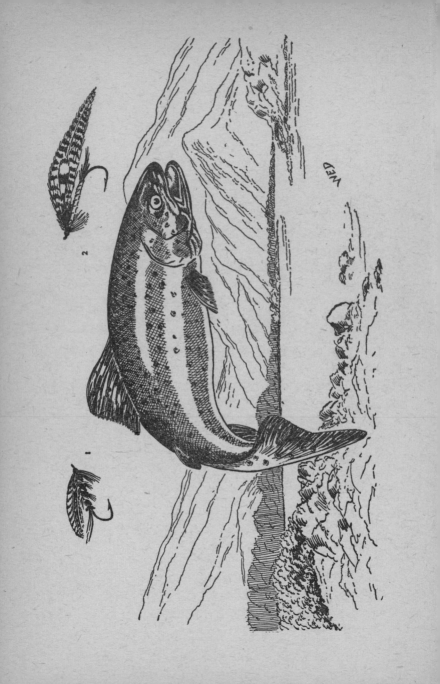

RAINBOW TROUT

How to Identify

I think this is the most colourful of the trouts. The back is olive green, overlaid with a sheen of gold and running along the sides is a beautiful pink streak with splashes of silver. The whole fish is covered with small brown, black and, on occasions, red spots. The head is small and the eyes large.

Habitat

An import from the mountain streams of America, this trout delights in fast streamy water and the more turbulent it is the better the rainbow likes it. It has been transplanted into lakes, but it is essentially a river fish. There are only a few rivers in this country where it is known to breed, the stock having to be kept up by planting each year. About a century ago the rainbow was looked upon as an ornament, something to beautify large ponds and lakes. Today it ranks with both the sea trout and salmon as a gamester, a fish that will test the best of men and tackle.

How to Catch

The rainbow will take fly, both wet and dry, and is partial to minnow, spoon, and spinning baits. In America

Illustration Key
  1. Wet fly
  2. American streamer fly

each year hundreds of large rainbows fall to the lure of the streamer fly, which was invented in the first place as a rainbow lure. There are many combinations of colours in streamers but the one which has usually found favour when I have been fishing is the Teal and silver, blue hackle and jungle cock cheeks.

An important factor when using streamers is that the cast must sink. Unless treated with a detergent or other substance, nylon floats and will buoy the fly near the surface. Natural silkworm gut is the best material for your 9-ft. terminal tackle. Fasten your streamer to the cast at least a couple of hours before starting to fish, then wrap the cast in coils and place them between folds of damp blotting paper, felt or other similar material. The gut will absorb enough moisture to make it sink on the first cast.

Sea trout lures are also acceptable to rainbows providing there is plenty of silver tinsel in the dressing.

Nature has provided this fish with a powerful body to withstand the pull of the fastest streams, where the current is strong there you will find your rainbow.

In lakes rainbows haunt out-jutting points of land, weed beds where there are plenty of small fish and the well-oxygenated water near islands. For lake fishing the flies range in size from No. 6 to No. 12, which is much larger than those normally used for river rainbows, the range of which is from No. 10 to No. 16.

When spinning work the bait slowly.

It is a most excellent table fish.

SALMON

HUNDREDS of thousands of words have been written about the salmon, but I think so far as description is concerned, one could not do better than to refer to this fish as one of Nature's greatest masterpieces. The name bestowed upon it by anglers the world over "King of Game Fish" is proof enough of the esteem it has engendered among the devotees of rod and line.

How to Identify

In fresh water it has four stages, the egg, fry, parr, and smolt. However, the angler is not interested from a catching point of view, in the smolt which is the young salmon on its way to the sea for the first time. But he is very much interested when it re-enters the river of its birth after a lapse of one to five years for it is then a grilse.

The coloration of a grilse is bright silver overlaid with a purplish sheen and with the tail slightly cleft. When it has spawned, returned to the sea and once more re-entered the river it is then a salmon proper. The coloration is slightly different. The silver is now overlaid with a metallic blue and the tail is square. There are no spots below the lateral line.

Between the grilse and salmon proper there is another stage which it behoves all anglers to identify, it is the

kelt period, a time when the salmon is, by Act of Parliament, deemed unclean. The Act, of course, also covers fish that are about to spawn.

The onus for correct decision rests with the angler concerned in every case, and the following characteristics by which unclean fish may generally be recognized are as follows:

Fish about to spawn (end of season). Outline unshapely, with increased depth of belly near vent. Males turn a reddish colour and the bottom jaw at the nose develops a hook or gib.

The belly of the female is more full and slight pressure on flanks in advanced cases may cause emission of ova (eggs).

Fish that have spawned and have not yet returned to the sea (kelts) are found usually during the opening weeks of a season. In shape they are emaciated, weight disproportionate to length, with distension or inflammation of vent. The fins are usually ragged as is also the tail. The colour is dark and dirty, but on occasions, especially with an early-spawned fish, it may be silvery, when other indications should be sought. The gills are a dirty pink instead of red and there are nearly always maggots present at the tips. In contrast to a fish from the sea a kelt's mouth is full of sharp teeth.

Bearing these facts in mind it is always best to tail your fish out at the early and latter part of a season.

Illustration Key
1. Devon
2. Fly

Habitat

Those rivers that are pure and having access to the sea.

How to Catch

Patience and still more patience is the keynote in all methods of luring salmon. In the spring natural bait including eel-tail, gold and silver sprat, minnow, and loach can be used with confidence, as can spinning artificials of the devon and spoon types.

When the water starts to clear the fly is indicated and can be used right through the season if need be. During May, June, and July a natural prawn, either spun or worked sink and draw in the runs and pools, will often take a fish or two when other methods have failed. With the water at summer level low-water flies (long-shanked hooks with small dressing) is a sporting method and one that accounts for a good many fish each year.

Always fish those pools and deep runs where there are plenty of sunken rocks. Salmon love these places for they can rest and recoup their strength while waiting for a flood to enable them to reach the upper sections of the river where the spawning beds (redds) are made.

For full details of catching salmon read *Salmon and Sea Trout Fishing* by W. E. Davies.

SEA TROUT

Local Names: **Sewen, Herling, Blackneb, White Trout, Salmon Trout, Peal, Whitling, Phinock**

How to Identify

The colour of this delightful migratory trout is a combination of blues, green, and silver with the back and sides well marked with small black spots. When fresh from the sea it is like a bar of living silver. It is a fish with many names. In England it is also known as herling, and whitling (Northumberland); peal (Devon and Cornwall); sewen (Wales); blackneb, herling, whitling and phinock (Scotland) and white trout (Ireland). Throughout the whole of these isles it is often referred to as salmon trout, this is no doubt due to its similarity to the salmon. In a young sea trout the tail is deeply forked but after it has spawned once the fork gradually disappears and the tail takes on the appearance of that of the salmon.

At times identification is most difficult. The holder of the British record for a rod-caught sea trout, Mr. S. R. Dwight, of Heath Farm, near Berkhamsted, Hertfordshire, a personal friend of mine, did not know he had caught a record sea trout until the scales had been read. All the so-called experts declared that the fish was a salmon. However, its captor had never seen a salmon with

so many spots below the lateral line, so the Editor of the *Fishing Gazette* arranged for a scale reading and the new record resulted.

Habitat

The sea trout is more or less a fish of the estuary for it never moves far from the mouth of a river. The majority of sea trout runs take place in April, May, and June, and by middle August they are well distributed in fresh water. During the hours of daylight they remain hidden and the angler has to work hard for a brace, but when darkness falls they move up into the flats and streams, there to feed on minnows, underwater insect life, and flies. They are friendly disposed to each other and move around in shoals, and those sections of a river where there is plenty of sand and shingle will always attract sea trout at night on account of the abundance of food and oxygen.

How to Catch

During daylight wet flies and also on occasions dry flies will lure an odd fish and if there is a fair depth of water a 1-in. blue and silver devon can be tried. In my opinion the blue and silver devon is the best artificial to use for sea-trout spinning. If there is a little colour in the water a fly-spoon can be tried. However, remember

---

Illustration Key

1. Fly spoon
2. Worm
3. Wet fly
4. Lure
5. Wet fly with maggots

the sea trout is wary so avail yourself of every bit of cover.

At night-time they are not so shy and it is then that the man who can cast a fly really comes into his own. In Devon and Cornwall anglers swear by lures. On the River Tavy it is the Peacock and silver and on several other rivers it is the blue and silver. A butcher friend of mine always uses a couple of maggots on his fly at night.

On quite a number of Scottish rivers the local anglers impale a docken grub on Pennell (two-hook) tackle and fish the streams by "swimming" the bait down. Worms are also fished in a similar way.

PART II

FRESHWATER FISH

Barbel
Silver Bream
Chub
Crucian Carp and
  Common Carp
Dace

Perch
Pike
Roach
Rudd
Tench

BARBEL

Local Names: **Freshwater Pig, Bearded Pig**

How to Identify

The back is greenish brown with the flanks yellowish green in colour. The head and gill covers appear as if they have been painted over with bronze. The belly is a dirty white. It has four fleshy beards which hang from the head, two being placed on the nose and the other two at each angle of the mouth.

Habitat

A mud-loving fish, it obtains its food by grubbing like a pig in among the roots of weeds and in the mud. The beards or barbules are believed to aid it in the search for food. It makes an abode always near the bank-side and where there is a good depth of water which must be on the sluggish side.

How to Catch

Barbel rank as the second heaviest fish in British waters, several reaching 14 lb. have been recorded. Angling for them is carried on during the summer and autumn months when the fish are far from being in the pink of condition, so this is no mean weight. I have no doubt that barbel of 18–20 lb. might be weighed-in if taken in February or early March.

Barbel were held in high repute during the reign of Queen Elizabeth when a statute was passed forbidding the taking of "barbels" under the size of 12 in. The penalty was "20 shillings", a considerable fine in those days. Incidentally so far as I know this Act has not been repealed.

Easy-running light ledger tackle is best to catch barbel. Do not be afraid to fish fine. Large lobworms, a bunch of brandling worms and plain bread-paste are good baits. The barbel is an epicure and has frequently fallen to a piece of fat pork the size of a sugar lump.

Ground-baiting calls for care. A quantity of the ordinary bread and bran variety should be worked up fairly stiff with a little clay to give it weight, and as an additional enticement a few chopped worms can be added to the mixture. The whole should be kneaded into the size of a cricket ball and thrown up-stream above the swim where the fish have been discovered.

In a short time this will draw them from the weeds to grub along the bottom to find what has been offered them.

Barbel fishing, however, calls for more patience than any other branch of angling.

The Thames, Trent, and Hampshire Avon are by far the best barbel rivers.

Best hook sizes are 6, 8, and 10. The barbel is not a recognized food fish.

Illustration Key

1. Knob of paste
2. Bunch of brandling worms
3. Lob worm

Illustration Key
1. Maggots
2. Paste
3. Worm

SILVER BREAM

Local Names: **White Bream, Tin Plate**

How to Identify

The mouth is small and the pelvic fins are tinged with red. The body is covered with mucus and the predominant colour is silver grey. It is of fairly wide distribution and is more at home in lakes and reservoirs.

How to Catch

The angler keen on making a good catch of silver bream should ground-bait heavily with small worms the swim he proposes to fish the following day. The bait should be a small red worm impaled as per illustration. Other well-known baits are a couple of maggots and bread-paste. It is not a sporting fish and once a shoal is located the angler who has taken the trouble to ground-bait overnight will be kept busy hauling them out.

The silver bream's near relative, the common or yellow bream, grows to a much larger size and one of the best-known spots in the British Isles are the reservoirs at Tring, Hertfordshire where several 12-pounders have been recorded. While roach rod and tackle are ideal for silver bream one needs a little heavier equipment for the yellow bream.

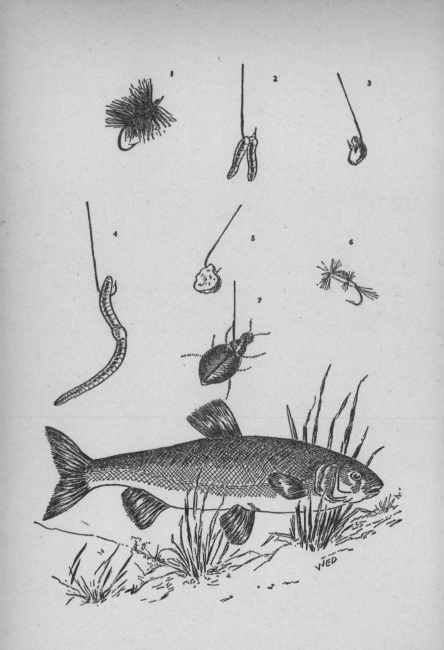

CHUB

Local Names: Chevin, Pollard, Bottling

How to Identify

Small chub are often mistaken for dace, but if the following note is kept in mind an angler will experience little difficulty. The ventral fins of the dace are greenish with a slight tinge of red. The anal fin has no red about it. In the chub both these fins are of a brilliant pink colour.

Habitat

Not so widely distributed as most freshwater fish, it delights in similar water to the trout and it is not an uncommon occurrence for a trout angler to catch chub when fly-fishing on rivers containing this species. The Rivers Avon and Stour are famous for chub. In the winter chub prefer deep water.

How to Catch

A very greedy fish, it feeds on insects, maggots, worms, paste, and in the summer will rise to artificial flies dressed palmer fashion. It is a cunning and exceedingly wary fish.

Illustration Key

1. Large palmer fly	5. Cheese
2. Maggots	6. Nymph
3. Paste	7. Beetle
4. Worm	

The angler must at all times take full advantage of every bit of cover. The advent of the fixed-spool reel and nylon monofilament has proved an untold blessing to the chub angler for he can with little effort fish fine and far off. One thing to bear in mind is that if the weather is fine, with the sun shining, chub will be cruising around near the surface. In cold, damp, and cloudy weather the fish will be browsing around near the bottom.

Large chub usually make their home under a big over-hanging tree, and wherever a caterpillar-infested tree or bush is located the water beneath will most probably hold a good chub or two. A powerful fighting fish for the first few minutes after the hook sinks home, the terminal tackle should never be less than 6-lb. breaking strain. The rod I use for chub is a 10-ft. split-cane sea trout fly-rod.

Due to the flesh containing an enormous quantity of hairlike bones the chub is not generally considered a table fish.

Hook sizes: paste, maggots and worm No. 10 Model Perfect. For insects No. 12 Crystal, and for artificial flies No. 12.

CRUCIAN CARP AND COMMON CARP

How to Identify

Crucian carp, unlike the common carp, has no barbels and its tail is less forked. It is not of such wide distribution as the common carp and a 4-pounder is considered a good fish. The predominant colours are bronze-green and yellow. Coloration, however, sometimes varies and on occasions I have seen crucian carp where the main colour was greenish-yellow.

The common carp is more bronze in its coloration and is not of such a chubby appearance. On the Continent carp have been recorded of 60-lb. weight but the largest rod-caught specimen in this country weighed 44 lb.

How to Catch

Both carps are shy and considerable patience has to be exercised by the angler who is after a specimen. Many carp anglers of my acquaintance fish during the hours of darkness and affix all manner of gadgets to their rods to tell them when a fish bites. Ground-baiting with worms or bread-crumbs should be undertaken some hours before the actual fishing takes place.

The crucian carp is not a great fighter but its larger relative puts up a hard fight for its freedom. It always

pays to let common carp take the bait with them for a few yards before striking. For crucian carp a roach rod is quite strong enough but for common carp the tackle must be capable of holding a fish that fights every inch of the way and very often has considerable weight to help it.

Good baits for both carps include lobworms, bread-paste in which honey has been mixed and bread-crust. Both species like sluggish water where there are plenty of weeds for cover.

Illustration Key

1. Crucian carp   4. Bread crust
2. Common carp   5. Lob worm
3. Knob of sweet paste

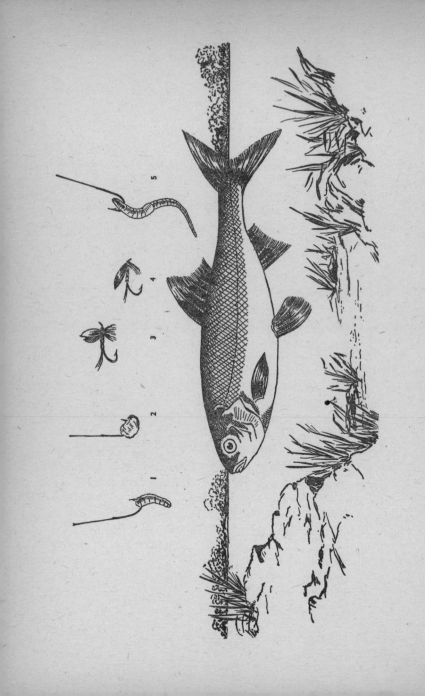

DACE

Local Names: **Dare, Dart**

How to Identify

The tail is small and very forked. The ventral fins are of a greenish hue tinged with red, the head is small and shapely and not of so blunt a formation as the chub.

Habitat

A lively little fish roaming around in shoals, it delights in streamy water and eddies near weed beds. It is of fairly wide distribution and a pound fish is considered a good one.

How to Catch

The same tackle as that used for roach and rudd can be used for dace, with the terminal tackle being a little finer. In the summer and early autumn artificial trout flies dressed on No. 16 hooks will usually interest dace. When they are moving around in a stream, "swimming" the bait down will be found to attract quite a few bites. The hook can be baited with small red worm, maggots or paste. The dace bites very quickly so at the least touch the angler should strike. Quill floats are considered best for dace when in deep water.

Illustration Key

1. Maggot   4. Wet fly
2. Paste   5. Worm
3. Dry fly

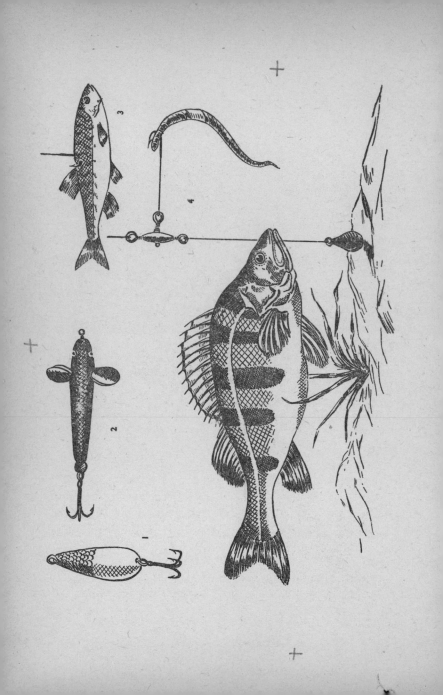

PERCH

How to Identify

This without a doubt is one of Nature's most colourful creations in these islands and is easily identified. The bronze-coloured back has usually six transverse bars of dark green bronze extending well down the flanks, while the whole is shaded with a lovely blue and green iridescence. The fins are covered with a tinge of red. The first dorsal fin is spiney and the tail is forked.

Habitat

Perch do not like swift water and much prefer to roam around in deep holes where there is plenty of cover from tree roots, overhung banks, etc. A predator, it levies a heavy toll amongst young fish. It is well distributed and some very fine specimens have been taken from Scottish lochs.

How to Catch

The three best methods of taking perch are, with the paternoster, spinning artificial baits, and by ledgering. Float-fishing is not so good as the other three. Best natural

---

Illustration Key

1. Semi-scaled silver spoon
2. Blue and silver devon
3. Live minnow
4. Paternoster with worm

baits are minnow and worm, but I have heard of some really good fish 3 lb. and over that have been caught on frogs. The illustration shows how to "bait-up" both minnow and worm. With ledger tackle the lead weight should not be too heavy for the bait must have freedom of movement and not be anchored to the bottom.

The best artificial baits for spinning are a $1\frac{1}{2}$-in. blue and silver devon and a 1-in. gold and silver semi-scaled spoon. Spinning baits are ideal for use in lakes where one can cover a lot of water. The paternoster is the proper tackle for searching out specimens in holes in rivers and canals and is quite easy to construct, see illustration.

PIKE

Local Names: **Freshwater Tiger, Water Wolf, Jack, Poor Man's Salmon, Tench's Friend**

How to Identify

Long body with forked tail, flat head with powerful jaws studded with shark-like teeth. The eye is large and resembles somewhat that of a falcon in colouring. Body is sometimes striped like a tiger, Scottish pike from deep lochs are very often marked this way, then again it may have splashes of golden bronze on its dark olive-green sides. The illustration is of such a fish. When in good condition the fins of a pike are tinged with red.

Habitat

At the edges of weed beds, behind rocks, holes in the banks or any other place from where it can pounce on its unsuspecting prey as it swims past. No matter what type of water, river or lake, the part which receives the most sun will hold the best pike, for this tyrant loves the sun and wherever possible makes a hide from where, in the summer, it can come forth and bask near the surface.

How to Catch

There are two schools of thought on this subject, one swears by live bait such as dace, roach, rudd, etc., and the other by artificials like spoons, devons, etc. However,

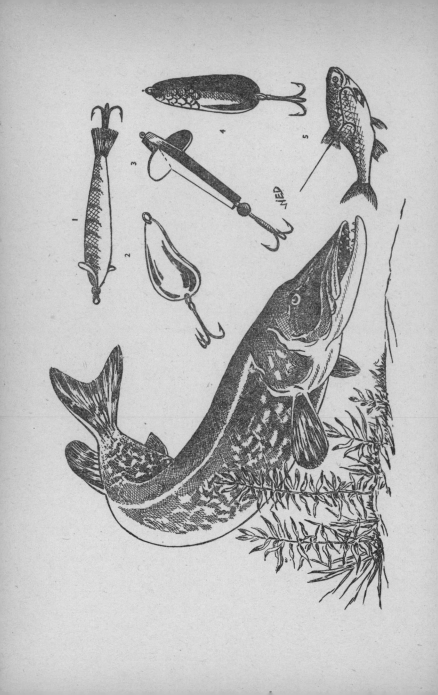

no matter what bait is used it should be connected to the line with about a foot length of 18-lb. to 20-lb. wire to offset the pike's powerful teeth which can shear through gut or nylon with ease.

The rod should be powerful, but not of the barge-pole variety or else the fish will be whipped before it has had a chance to show what it is really capable of. Indeed, both in Scotland and Ireland, I have had pike leap out of the water like any salmon.

If spinning, work the bait slowly, more fish have been lost through turning the reel handle fast than have ever been caught. When a fish takes hold let him move off with the bait a few yards before striking, then hit him hard as the inside of his mouth is sheathed in bone.

For live-baiting I have always found the Jardine Snap Tackle to be best.

It is an excellent food fish and in the reign of Henry VIII was more valuable than salmon.

There are more legends about this fish than any other, or should I say more lies have been told. The greatest fabrication of all is of course that about the pike recorded to have lived 260 years and to have been over 300 lb. in weight.

Illustration Key

1. Featherow minnow
2. Heavyweight silver spoon
3. Reflex devon
4. Silver and gold semi-scaled spoon
5. Live bait

ROACH

How to Identify

A member of the carp family, the roach is often mistaken for a rudd and vice versa. However, there is one feature which makes it easy to distinguish it from its near relative. It is the dorsal fin which is set only slightly behind the pelvic fin. In the rudd the dorsal is well behind the pelvic. Another point is that the mouth in the roach is much smaller. Yet another characteristic of the roach is that the eye iris is a beautiful deep red colour and in the rudd it is a metallic yellow and finally the red colour on the tips of the fins is more pronounced in the rudd.

Habitat

The more sluggish a water the better roach like it providing there are plenty of weed beds about. The canals which criss-cross the southern half of England are mostly full of roach, while reservoirs and lakes generally have a good head. In rivers and canals it feeds at the edges of eddies formed by rocks, weed beds, etc.

How to Catch

On occasions roach are imbued with great cunning

Illustration Key

1. Maggot
2. Hempseed
3. Paste
4. Small red worm

which makes them exceedingly difficult to lure and at other times they exhibit suicidal tendencies, when they are easy to capture. Prior to the First World War the usual baits were paste (various kinds), maggots, bread-flake, boiled wheat and worms, but with the arrival of many Belgians for munition work a new bait made its appearance. This was hempseed a well-known bait on the Continent. Since arrival in this country "hemp" as it is usually called, has accounted for some really fine specimens.

Very sensitive float tackle is the usual method of taking roach, but on occasions when the fish are well down ledger equipment with a bait of paste or worm can be quite good. Many roach anglers use maggots and paste of different colours, but from talks I have had with recognized experts at roach fishing ordinary bread-paste and natural-coloured maggots are just as good.

As in baits so in ground-baiting, for many anglers abide by their own secret formulas, mixing in with the bread-crumbs, biscuit, etc., various essences which it is claimed lure the fish to the baited hook. Be that as it may the angler who relies on a ground-bait mixture of dried bread-crumbs and very small maggots, moistened and worked into a paste will not go far wrong. Ground-baiting can be overdone, the idea being to attract the fish, not to feed them, so pieces about the size of a hazel-nut flipped in slightly above where the baited hook is are quite large enough.

Regarding floats, the one most in evidence on the following famous roach rivers, Thames, Avon, and Stour and the majority of canals and lakes, is the quill in various sizes to suit the water.

Of course most anglers have their own ideas on floats and what they should be capable of. Some anglers collect floats like some trout anglers collect flies and as a result spend most of their time changing one or the other. Cut down on the number of floats and you will have more fishing time.

For those who are handy with tools float-making is an interesting hobby and adds to the thrill of catching fish.

The roach is not recognized as a food fish but in some parts of the country it is considered a tasty dish when caught during the winter months.

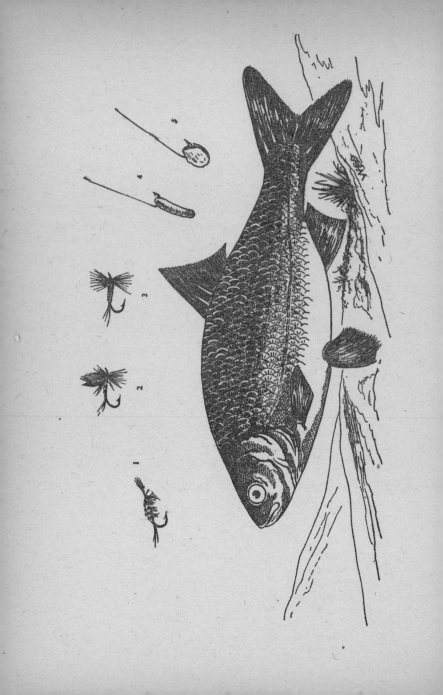

RUDD

How to Identify

In the pages dealing with the roach will be found the necessary information on how to differentiate between rudd and roach.

Habitat

Of not such a wide distribution as the roach this species is very plentiful in the Norfolk Broads. Where the water is shallow the rudd's coloration is very often bright golden, while in deep water its colouring is similar to that of a roach.

How to Catch

The methods, baits, etc., given for the luring of roach also apply to rudd with this addition. In summer and early autumn it can be taken consistently on artificial trout flies No. 16 wet or dry. Artificial nymphs and shrimps are also good on occasions when the fish are nosing among the weeds.

Illustration Key

1. Artificial shrimp
2. Winged dry fly
3. Spider dry fly
4. Maggot
5. Bread flake

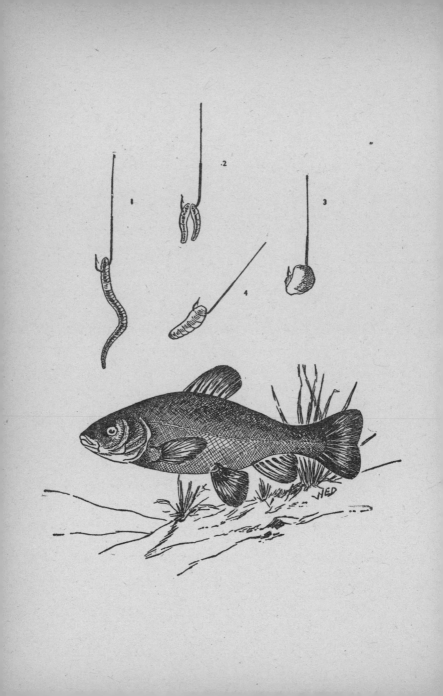

TENCH

Local Names: **Doctor Fish, Pike's Friend**

How to Identify

The general colour is dark olive green overshot with grey which at times makes the fish look black. The whole body, when the fish is in good condition, is covered with a thick slime or mucus.

Habitat

It is a bottom-feeding fish much preferring those parts where there is plenty of mud and weeds and where the water is sluggish. It is particularly active during early summer when the atmosphere is humid. When the autumn sets in and the temperature falls it hibernates in the mud to await the return of the spring sun. Occasionally tench are caught in winter, but only on rare occasions has this happened.

How to Catch

In their feeding tench root about among the roots of weeds and in the mud, and very often their feeding locality can be detected by a stream of little air bubbles that

---

Illustration Key

1. Lob worm
2. Maggot
3. Knob of paste
4. Wasp grub

appear on the surface of the water. Of course a stream of bubbles coming to the surface does not necessarily mean that a tench is feeding, as it may well be gas escaping from the rotting vegetation on the bed of the water. But whenever such bubbles are noticed it is always wise to have a try.

Lobworms, brandling worms and red worms are usually the baits that account for the biggest fish. However some really fine specimens have fallen to the lure of maggots, paste and wasp-grub.

The best time of the day to fish for them is very early morning on a summer's day just as it is breaking daylight. It is not a recognized fish for the table.

At one time it was thought the pike was disposed to be friendly with the tench, as the slime on the latter's body was a cure to all the ills that might befall a pike, but like so many other things regarding the pike it is just a legend for the pike makes friends with no one—not even members of its own family.

Best hooks to use are No. 8, 10 or 12 Model Perfect.

PART III

SALTWATER FISH

The Angler Fish
Bass
Black Bream
Coalfish
Haddock and Cod
Conger Eel
Flounder
Garfish
Grey Mullet

Ling
Mackerel
Plaice
Pollack
Skate
Sting Ray
Thornback Skate
The Weaver and
    Greater Weaver
Whiting

THE ANGLER FISH

How to Identify

If when bottom fishing you should catch a fish that appears to be all head and mouth, with long waving spines half-way down its back and a dirty brown in colour, it is ten to one that your capture is the angler fish. The pectoral fins are large and look more like feet. With these fins the angler digs a hole in the sand, the spines along its back wave to and fro with the movement of the water, and when a fish comes along to inspect what it is the angler just opens its mouth and there is one less fish in the sea.

It is a species that is often taken when autumn-fishing for more valuable fish. A perfect glutton it can spoil one's fishing in that it has the ability to take fish off the angler's hooks time and again without being caught itself.

Habitat

In areas frequented by dog fish it grows to a large size. This is no doubt due to the fact that these small sharks are of a more inquisitive nature than most fish. One 40-lb. angler fish, caught in a Cornish fisherman's net, which the writer examined had nine dog fish inside it including three spur dogs. There were also a couple of small crabs and some partly digested whiting.

It usually prefers deep water (30 to 40 fathoms) and can be said to be fairly common off the south and west coasts.

Until a few years ago commercial fishermen used to use it for baiting long lines to catch other fish. Today it is skinned and finds a ready sale under quite a number of attractive names.

BASS

Local Names: **White Salmon, Salmon Dace, Sea Perch, Poor Man's Salmon, The Wolf**

How to Identify

This species is easily identified by its two dorsal fins, the first being strong and composed of nine spinous rays of which the angler should be wary when removing the hook as they can make a nasty wound if handled carelessly. The second dorsal has thirteen rays. The tail is slightly forked and built on robust lines.

Shoulders and back are silvery-grey with flanks and belly silvery-white. The colouring is no doubt responsible for the "salmon" tag in the local names one meets from time to time.

Habitat

The bass is present around the south and west coasts of England all the year, but the greatest concentration is during the summer and autumn months. Feeding on smaller fish, shrimps and shellfish they prefer a rocky shoreline, interspersed with sandy beaches. Wherever there are sand-eels there you will find the most bass as this fish forms the major portion of its diet.

While small bass (schoolers) fish of $\frac{1}{2}$ lb. to 2 lb. are in evidence throughout the whole year, fish of 5 lb. and

upwards are migratory in habit. They arrive in coastal waters from the deeps about June, moving off again in November. While a number of large bass have been taken by shore anglers in recent years the man who fishes from a boat always has the best chance of reeling in a specimen.

How to Catch

For beach casting the bait should be cast beyond the third breaker and with the fixed-spool reels now on the market this is quite easy. Seven of the best natural baits are illustrated showing method of mounting.

Artificial baits include first and foremost, rubber eels of varying colours, red, black, green or white, silver and gold spoons, devons of gold and silver, and wagtails. With wagtails the best colour combination I have found is blue and silver.

Here is a list of the best-known bass stations:

Kent Coast: Broadstairs, Dover, Folkestone, Herne Bay, Margate, Ramsgate.

Sussex Coast: Bognor, Brighton, Eastbourne, Hastings, Littlehampton, Newhaven, Seaford.

Hampshire: Bournemouth, Christchurch.

Dorset: Bridport, Poole, Weymouth.

Devon: Brixham, Dartmouth, Exmouth, Ilfracombe, Plymouth, Salcombe, Seaton, Sidmouth, Torcross, Torquay.

Cornwall: Coverack, Falmouth, Looe, Mevagissey, Penzance, Polperro, St. Ives, Sennen Cove.

Wales: Aberdovey, Anglesey, Carnarvon, Barmouth, Pwllheli, Swansea, Tenby.

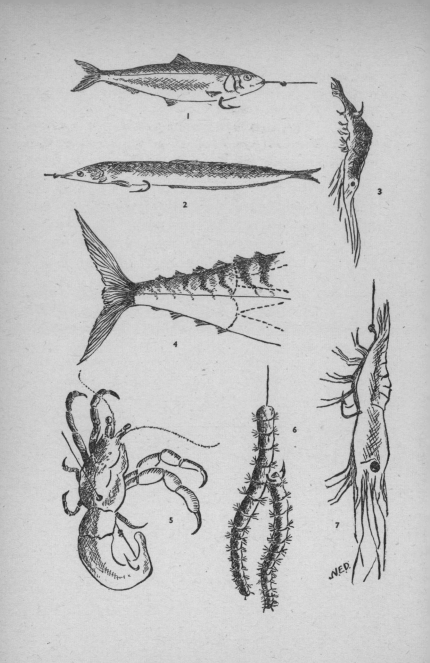

Bass

Ireland: Ballycotton, Baltimore, Bantry, Cork Harbour, Kinsale, Youghal, Waterville, Ardnore, Carnsore, Kilmore Quay, Wexford, Dunkineely.

The bass is an excellent food fish providing it is eaten within twenty-four hours of its being caught. It can of course be preserved a little longer if one has a fridge.

Illustration Key

Seven of the best natural baits for Bass

1. Pilchard
2. Sand-eel
3. Shrimp
4. Mackerel Lask
5. Hermit Crab
6. Ragworm
7. Prawn

BLACK BREAM

Local Name: **Old Wife**

How to Identify

The word black is a misnomer because there is nothing sombre about the coloration of this species. The cock is a real gaudy fellow, with his purples, blues, gold, silver, and bronze worked together as only Nature can. The hen is not quite so brilliantly attired, her principal colours being silver and grey. The mouth is small and the long, deep dorsal fin is composed of very sharp spines, as a result the fish needs careful handling when the hook is being removed.

How to Catch

This bream (there are several species) is a visitor from the Mediterranean and usually appears off the south and west coasts about April and stays for three or four months for the purpose of spawning. It prefers depths of 5 to 12 fathoms where there are plenty of rocks and weeds. Drift-lining with one hook is considered the best of methods, with float-fishing second. Lugworm and

---

Illustration Key

1. Lugworm
2. Piece of herring flesh

mackerel flesh are the best baits and ground-baiting with boiled rice is advisable once a shoal has been located.

Like some flat fish the black bream sucks the bait into its mouth, so the hook must be on the small side. Long-shanked dab hooks are what many good bream anglers use. Jardine spiral leads are the best weights to use for drift-lining as the sizes can easily be altered to suit the rise and fall of the tide. A fine day, rising tide and a well-anchored boat and the angler is assured of a pleasant time.

COALFISH

Local Names: **Sillock, Saithe, Pitlock, Harbin, Sethe, Grey Lord, Greenland Cod, Podling, Billet**

How to Identify

The coalfish is often referred to as the fish with a hundred names. Every locality and country seems to have found a different name for it. On occasions coalfish are mistaken for pollack, but there are three very distinct differences between the species. First the lateral line in a coalfish consists of a series of white dots and dashes. The lateral line of a pollack is a dirty green in colour. Secondly the coalfish on first being taken from the water is a lovely dark blue on the back, shading to a dirty white on the belly. After death the dark blue changes to black. The coloration of the pollack is bronze and olive green. Lastly the under jaw of the pollack is considerably longer than the upper jaw, while the jaws of the coalfish are practically level.

How to Catch

Of fairly wide distribution round our coasts, the coalfish is a strong fighter and is built for speed. When hooked it fights it out near the surface.

When they are on the feed the gulls and terns give the location very quickly as they fly about, diving here and

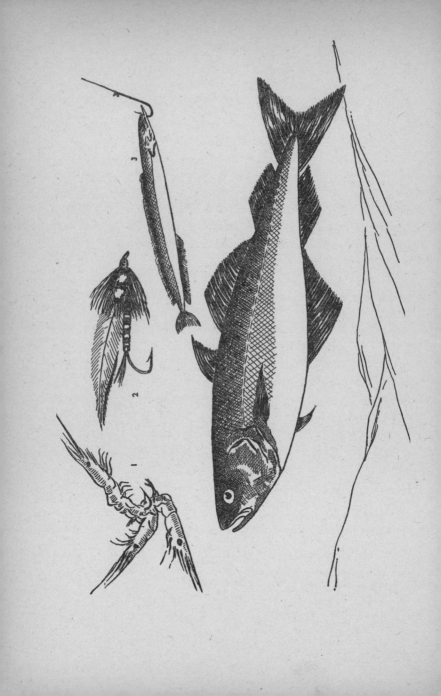

there to snatch the maimed and dying fish fry left in the wake of the slashing coalfish. Once a school has been located and one is fishing from a boat there is nothing to equal the sport derived from fly-fishing. One can troll or cast to the fish from an anchored boat.

The fly should be of the largest salmon size, which is about 3¼ in. long No. 10, and have plenty of colour in its dressing with a silver tinsel body. The fly is dressed streamer-fashion, the long hackle feathers being either bright red, blue or orange, the large hackle wound at the head is always yellow with a jungle-cock feather on either cheek.

A 14-ft. salmon fly-rod is a nice tool to use for casting to the fish, but for trolling a light boat-rod of 8 ft. will be ideal, or one can use a salmon-spinning rod.

The general run of fish on the fly is from 6 to 12 lb. although a friend of mine once had a 16-pounder from Loch Torridon (Scotland) when trolling, and for a time thought he was fast to a salmon.

For the really big fish there is nothing to beat trolling with a large red rubber eel, say one of 9 in. to 1 ft. in length. Shrimps and sand eels are good natural trolling baits. See illustration.

Illustration Key
1. Bunch of shrimps
2. Streamer fly
3. Sand-eel

HADDOCK AND COD

How to Identify

These two species are linked together because they inhabit similar localities, and methods of catching and baits used are the same. The haddock is easily identified by the black "thumb" mark on the shoulder and the soft spiney first dorsal fin. Both fish have barbels but that of the cod is the bigger. Colour of the haddock is greyish-brown merging into white, the lateral line is black. Coloration of the cod is a combination of olive green and brown with dark marbled markings above and below the lateral line. When freshly caught the back and flanks of a cod are suffused with a gold colour. This quickly fades.

How to Catch

Both species feed fairly deep and the best tackle is a three-boomed paternoster of brass or stainless steel. While the haddock does not run to a great size, a 4- or

---

Illustration Key

1. Haddock
2. Cod
3. Bottom hook of three-boom paternoster baited with a piece of herring

5-pounder is a good one, the cod is known to reach weights exceeding 30 lb., hence the need for stout tackle, including a powerful rod. Neither fish is shy and neither puts up a fight. Both are good food fish.

Baits include fish flesh, mussels, cockles, lug, and ragworm.

CONGER EEL

How to Identify

Coloration on the back varies from nearly black to slate-grey with the flanks and belly usually a dirty white with an occasional greenish tinge. Large congers are always the females, males usually average about 4 lb. The jaws and teeth are of powerful construction.

How to Catch

The habitat of this sea eel is the rocky bottom where during the day-time the really big girls remain concealed in some hole or crevice of a rock, to come forth at dusk in search of food. Where wrecks are is one of the best places to get a specimen. A piece of cuttle fish is a very good bait although many 50- and 60-pounders have fallen to fillets of mackerel, herring or pouting. The essential thing is that the bait must be fresh. An excellent idea is to catch your bait during the day for a night's conger fishing then you know it is absolutely fresh.

The best rods are made of split cane, double built and, while powerful, not too stiff. The reel for such a rod should be a 5 or 6 in., capable of holding 120 yards of 40- or 50-lb. braided nylon. An important feature of any reel is the handle and for this eel the handle should be large to assist in quick reeling, because if the conger is given a

chance to get his tail around a rock or anything else handy the battle is going to be a long-drawn-out business.

A wire trace is essential and my preference is for a 2-ft. soft nickel-chrome twisted wire. The hooks range from 6/0 to 11/0, according to the bait used and the swivel should be attached to the hook, see illustration. There should be a couple of free-working swivels in the trace.

The gaff should be lashed to the handle, a gaff-head which screws in to the handle is a menace when conger fishing at night, as invariably when the conger is on the surface and the gaff goes home, it starts twisting around and this is no treatment for a gaff-head that screws in. Many a good fish, together with gaff-head, has been lost as a result.

Always keep the hooks needle sharp with an occasional rub on emery cloth or "stone" and on a moonless night take a good electric torch with you and a spare gaff just to be on the safe side.

Illustration Key
1. Gaff lashed to handle
2. Conger hook

FLOUNDER

Local Names: **White Fluke, Black Flat Fish (Wales)**

How to Identify

Main coloration is brown with darker patches which occasionally merge into black each side of the lateral line. The underside in a freshly caught fish is a beautiful, pearly white. The wrist to the tail is longer and more slender than the plaice.

How to Catch

Of very wide distribution the flounder flourishes in salt, brackish or fresh water, and prefers those areas where there are both sand and mud patches. The two baits considered by many anglers to stand above all others are the two sea worms, lug and rag. As the tide advances up an estuary, disturbing the mud and bringing out the ragworms, there you will find flounders, and at the mouth of an estuary along the sand-stretches the flounders hunt the lugworms.

Several large flounders have been recorded as having been caught on spoon and a few on devon, but by and large natural bait will always take more flounders than artificials.

Illustration Key
1. Lugworm

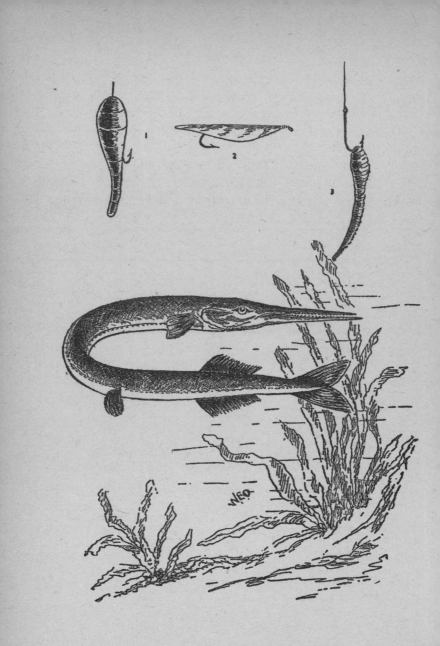

Garfish

A good food fish, it is grand eating and in flavour is not unlike plaice, but because of its green bones many anglers throw it away or use it for bait to catch other fish. Granted it makes an excellent bait but I much prefer to eat it myself.

It rarely attains a large size and a 30-in. fish is considered a good one. The illustration is of a 22-in. fish weighing nearly 2 lb. taken by the author at Littlehampton while fishing for black bream.

Illustration Key
1. Tail of hermit crab
2. Mackerel skin tied to hook
3. Lugworm

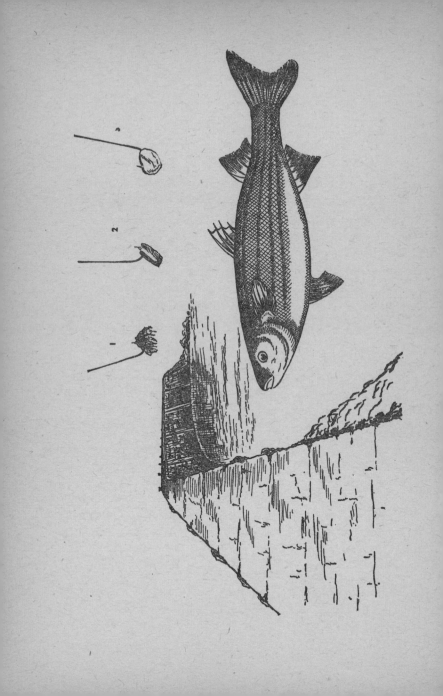

GREY MULLET

How to Identify

One of the first indications that spring and warmer weather is not far off is the appearance in the south and west coastal waters of shoals of grey mullet. The colour of the back is silver and grey, the belly is silvery-white and on the sides are a number of lines of a rosy-brown. A smallish mouth with fairly thick lips, it has small teeth and relies on speed and cunning to outwit its enemies. It has two dorsal fins, the first having four or five spines.

How to Catch

The wariest of fish, to catch grey mullet consistently, and believe me it can be done, the motto of the angler at all times should be, "Hurry slowly." To defeat this grey and silver quarry, just as much care is required in the preparation of the bait as in selection of the right tackle.

Mullet delight in such places as wharves, jetties, barges, sea-walls, piers, harbours, and estuaries. Best results are obtained when the tide is from half-flood to high-water,

---

Illustration Key

1. Green weed
2. Boiled macaroni
3. Bread paste

after which the fish move out with the tide. As the season advances, with a rise in temperature, they move up into the estuaries and it is then that the summer angler gets his chance.

My favourite type of hook is a No. 10 short-shank Model Perfect and while there are numerous baits known to have taken mullet the angler who pins his faith in boiled macaroni or bread-paste will not go far wrong.

To bring a shoal on to feed, a cloud bait, which, as it disintegrates, will keep the fish interested without feeding them is made with bran that has been roasted in the oven and crushed oatmeal biscuits.

I like a 9-ft. trout fly-rod for mullet work but my son swears by his 12-ft. roach-rod which has a split-cane top.

In the preparation of baits make perfectly sure that your hands are clean and minus nicotine stains and when fishing take advantage of every bit of cover available. For quiet estuaries float-tackle can be good, but for pier, harbour wall, and wharf fishing "swimming" down minus the float will usually take a fish or two.

The hook tackle should never be more than 5-lb. breaking strain and the running line 4 or at most 6 lb. heavier. The grey mullet fights hard, so take your time; at the first signs of distress use your net and so prevent undue splashing which would alarm the rest of the shoal.

LING

How to Identify

The colouring is a blended combination of browns, yellows, and whites. The back is a light yellow and brown, marbled with yellow and brown, and over all a number of golden-brown bars. On some of the bars there is considerable mottling of gold. The belly is white. Tail is round and edged with white as is also the case with the dorsal and anal fins.

Habitat

This, one of the most valuable of food fish, favours fairly deep water and is rarely caught in depths under 50 fathoms. In the whole of my fifty years angling I have caught only three. They were taken off the Ross-shire coast of Scotland, while fishing for haddock. All three were just over the 6-lb. mark.

Scientists claim the ling to be the most prolific of all fish. Many of the deep Scottish sea lochs are well populated with this species and large catches are made in the autumn and winter. It grows to a large size, particularly in the waters around the Hebrides where 30-pounders are common.

In the old days of a century ago the crofters on the coast of Scotland's far north valued this fish above all others from the sea. The oil from its liver was used to

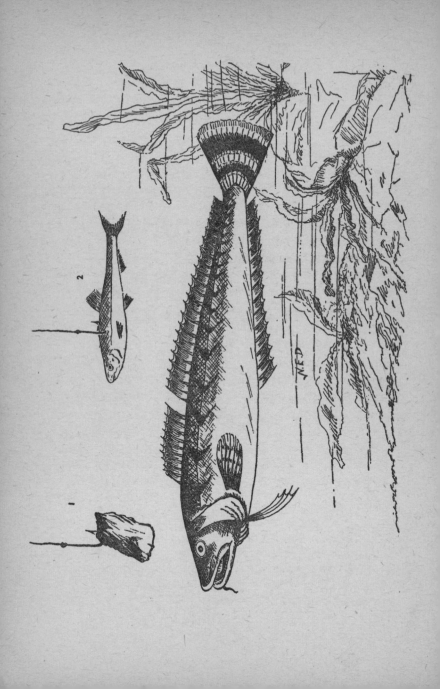

burn in the lamps and it was also used as a remedy for all manner of muscular aches and pains. Even today in many of the off-the-beaten-track sea hamlets and villages "ling-oil" is the recognized cure for rheumatism.

How to Catch

Whenever one visits Scotland for a sea-fishing holiday it is always advisable to put a large cod hook on the bottom boom of the paternoster just in case a ling happens to be roaming in the vicinity. However, remember this fish likes deep water and a 7- or 8-in. reel is advisable to facilitate quick reeling in. Make sure that such a reel has large handles or else your fingers and wrists are going to suffer.

The best baits are large pieces of mackerel, herring, and cod flesh and live whiting.

The crofters catch ling on long lines to which are attached one hundred or more large hooks, these are laid one evening and taken in the following evening. Like a number of other species of sea fish, the ling feeds largely at night.

Illustration Key
1. Piece of mackerel
2. Live bait

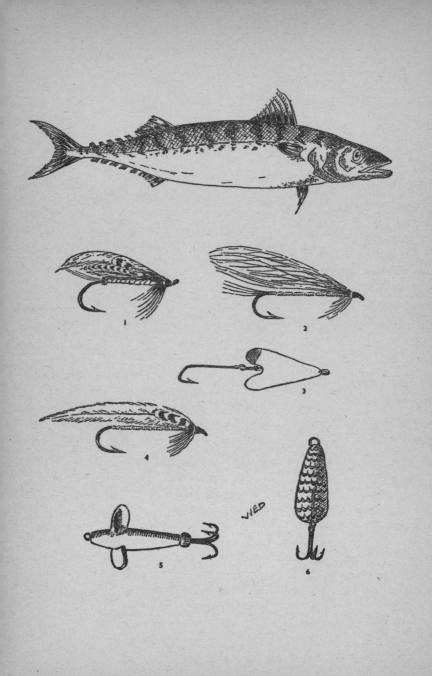

MACKEREL

How to Identify

To my way of thinking this is one of the most brightly coloured of our sea fish, the iridescence of the wavy bands on the back are beyond my powers of description. The lateral line comes above the pectoral fins. There are two dorsal fins and five, six or seven finlets from the second dorsal to the tail.

How to Catch

An offshoot of the tunny family, the mackerel is among the gamest of our small inshore fish. A 4-lb. nylon trace or fly cast and a 6-lb. running line and the angler will really enjoy himself when mackerel are in. All manner of artificial baits will attract and gaudy coloured flies, salmon and streamer patterns, will produce plenty of sport when the fish are working near the surface. Spinning with devons and spoons can be indulged in when the mackerel are close in shore which is usually during mid-summer. Trolling from a boat with a cast of two or three flies is a good way to spend an hour or two on a sunny day.

Illustration Key

1. Salmon fly
2. Hair fly
3. Mackerel spoon
4. Streamer fly
5. Devon
6. Scale-back spoon

When they are feeding, deep lug and ragworm and the usual fish flesh will always take a fish or two. A 3-in. slice of skin 1 in. wide from a freshly caught mackerel and put on the hook of a mackerel spoon, trolled or worked sink and draw is also a very deadly bait. The only trouble with this particular bait is that if it is allowed to get down too deep one attracts small pollack so, bearing this in mind, the lead weight should not be too heavy.

However, to return to the question of flies. Years ago mackerel flies were heavy, cumbersome things, but today they have been slimmed down, what is more most of the creations for mackerel fishing consist of half a dozen three or four-inch cock-hackle feathers tied to a long-shanked hook and are known in fishing circles as "feathers".

Christmas time is the period to collect feathers as I have found that poultry dealers are only too pleased to get rid of the feathers which accumulate at this time of the year. White feathers are the best to collect, then they can be dyed any colour you wish. Incidentally colours which lure above all others are: Blue, yellow, red and plain white. When making your flies mix the colours together so that you have one or more of each colour to a fly.

Always remember that cold weather drives mackerel down to the deeps and warm spells bring them near the surface. The reason being that the fish fry, shrimps, etc.—upon which they feed—move about near the surface during periods of rising temperature.

If the angler gives an occasional glance at the sea-gulls he will soon know when the mackerel are on the move, for whenever mackerel feed near the surface there you will find these birds in large numbers wheeling, diving and screaming as if they were actually endeavouring to attract the attention of all anglers in the vicinity to come and have a go.

Places noted for large mackerel, that is fish over two pounds, include the Cornish coast and the water off Peel, Isle of Man.

PLAICE

How to Identify

This is one of our most valuable flat fish and is easily recognized by the large red spots on the upper side of the body.

How to Catch

It delights in those areas where there is plenty of gravel and sand and the angler who can find such a place in which there are plenty of mussel brood (young mussels) is always assured of a plaice supper.

Baits include lug and ragworms and small pieces of fish flesh. The hooks should be small, those used for dab fishing are ideal and long shanks are best because the plaice invariably gets the bait well down.

General tackle is the same as that used for flounders.

Illustration Key
  1. Ragworm
  2. Lugworm

POLLACK

How to Identify

Colour in general is a beautiful bronze and olive green and when the fish is first caught the colours shimmer and appear to be translucent. The lateral line is a dirty green colour and the bottom jaw is longer than the top one, a characteristic which is present throughout the life of the fish.

How to Catch

At most times of the year greedy and voracious, the pollack will strike equally well at all manner of baits, mussel, lug, ragworm, mackerel lask and the usual fish flesh, artificial flies, rubber eels, spoon, devon, and wagtail. Wherever there are submerged rocks and plenty of sea vegetation there you will find pollack.

The fish is not so great a fighter as the coal fish, but gives a good account of himself when hooked on light tackle. When they are really on the feed a cast of three mackerel flies worked sink and draw will usually levy a heavy toll. The secret in successful pollack fishing is to keep the bait on the move—slowly. A salmon spinning-rod is ideal.

Illustration Key
1. Rubber sand-eel
2. Double mackerel lask
3. Lugworm

113

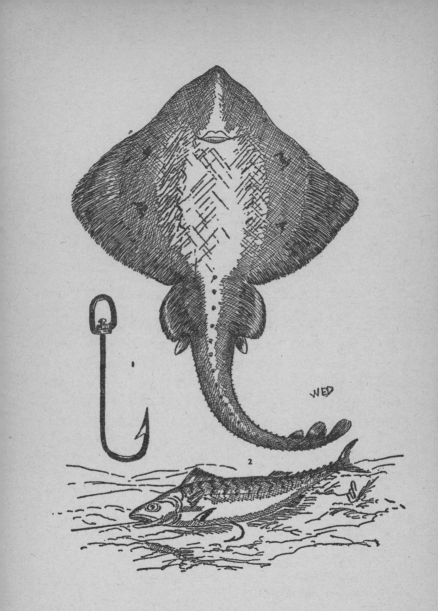

SKATE

How to Identify

This member of the ray family can be identified by its bluish-white underside which is more pronounced than in any of the other rays. The human-like mouth is also more defined.

How to Catch

In the first place the rod and tackle should be of the strongest, for 100-lb. fish are not uncommon, especially off the Irish coast. Mackerel flesh is considered the best bait, but it must be fresh. A strong wire trace and a large hook in which the swivel is incorporated is essential. Sand and gravel areas are usually the best places to find real specimens.

They prefer depths of 8 to 15 fathoms, indeed a couple of 160-lb. Irish skate I saw caught came from only 6 fathoms.

Illustration Key
> Underside of skate showing human-like mouth
> 1. Hook for skate
> 2. Mackerel impaled for skate

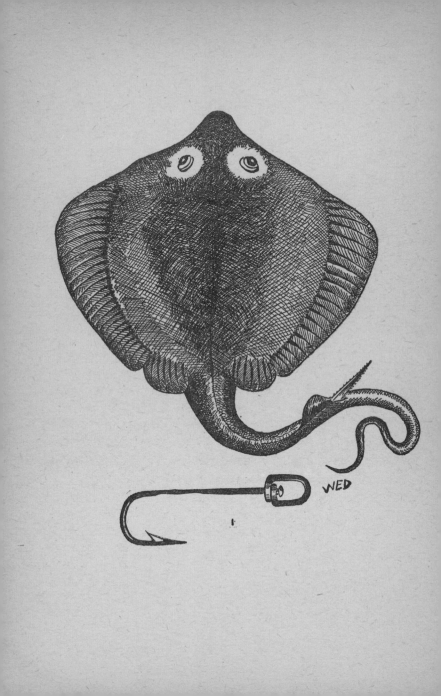

STING RAY

How to Identify

The ray family is a very large one, but the sting ray is one of the easiest to identify due to the arrow-shaped spine on the tail. Coloration is a combination of greys and browns.

How to Catch

A bottom feeder, like most of the other rays, it is usually caught when you are after skate. It prefers mackerel flesh to all others and is a dour fighter when hooked; as in all ray fishing a hook in which the swivel is incorporated is best and the trace must be of strong wire, 2 ft. long with a couple of free-working swivels is just right.

Warning. Always exercise the greatest care when handling a sting ray for the arrow in its tail is a deadly weapon and can inflict a serious wound.

Illustration Key
  I. Hook for sting ray

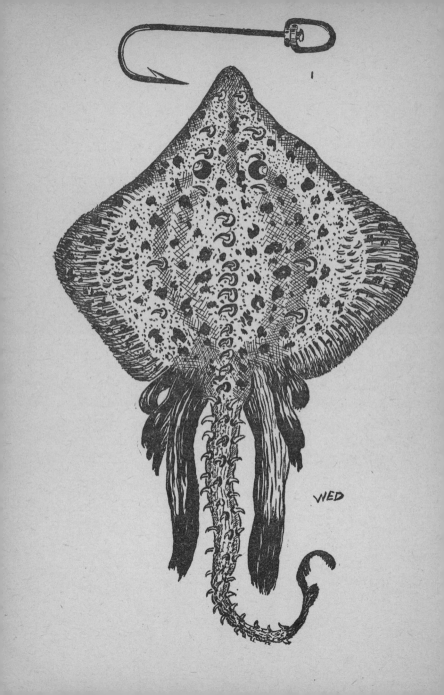

THORNBACK SKATE

How to Identify

This is the most common of the ray family round our coasts. It is of fairly easy identification due to the spines or thorns which are in evidence on the upper side. General coloration is brown and grey and in very large specimens there are brown marbled markings on the back.

How to Catch

It is often caught when bottom fishing for other species and like most of the ray family it is partial to fresh mackerel. There are great numbers of these fish on the south coast of England and the anglers who go after them use skate hooks and wire traces as their jaws are very powerful. It does not grow to such a large size as the skate and its flesh is not so good to eat, being more coarse. Like the skate it prefers shallow water.

Illustration Key
  I. Hook for thornback

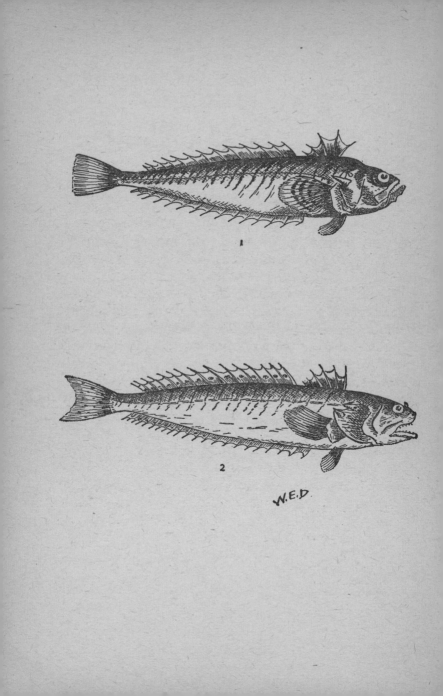

1

2

W.E.D.

THE WEAVER AND GREATER
WEAVER

Local Names: **Sting Fish, Sting Bull, Viper Fish,
Serpent Hound**

No one fishes for this species, although very often it is
caught when fishing for dabs from a pier or rocks. That
being so a general description will suffice.

Life for most creatures of the sea is one great struggle,
where those who put to the best use the strength and
abilities conferred upon them have, as a rule, most success.
The conditions of the game are fixed, but the powers and
qualities used in the struggle vary a little. Poison, spines of
needle-sharpness and claws that would do justice to a
carnivore, together with skill and endurance alike, have
their part to play and each competitor, if he hopes to go
on living, is called upon to do his best.

Nature has equipped both the fish, here illustrated with
poison glands and also needle-sharp spines, and each is
well able to take care of itself in the great struggle for life.

Sketch No. 1 is of the weaver most common to our
coasts. It is often referred to as the lesser weaver to
distinguish it from its larger relative.

Illustration Key
1. Weaver
2. Greater Weaver

It rarely exceeds 5 in. in length and is brownish-yellow in colour the back being mottled with yellow, while the flanks are covered with brown streaks and bars.

Warning. The spines on the dorsal fin can inflict a nasty wound to the unwary, but the most dangerous part of this fish is the head, for on the upper part of the gill covers are spines which lie flat when the fish is at rest, but come out at right angles when it is alarmed. It is these that are dangerous.

They are shaped like a grooved bayonet and along these grooves the poison travels from the sacs at their base. There are at least two cases of death on record as having been caused from the virus of this fish.

The best way to deal with a weaver is to kill it by putting your foot down pretty hard on the head. When dead the "poison bayonets" lie flat against the gill covers and the hook can then be removed.

If you are fishing in weaver-inhabited waters carry a little bottle of Scrubbs ammonia with you and should you be unfortunate enough to get stung, sponge the wound frequently with it. This will hold the inflammation in check and greatly reduce the pain. It is always best to see a doctor as quickly as possible.

The greater weaver is a rare visitor to our waters, it is much larger and more yellow in colour.

WHITING

How to Identify

This is one member of the cod family which is minus a barbel. Coloration is silvery with a sheen of gold on the back and when first caught there are a number of faint gold markings running from the dorsal fins to the well-defined lateral line. These markings disappear at death. There is also a black spot above the root of the pectoral fin.

How to Catch

So far as is known at present the largest whiting are located off the coast of Ross-shire, Scotland, near the village of Shieldaig. The fishing takes place in two sea lochs, Loch Shieldaig and Loch Torridon. The largest whiting ever to be caught on rod and line came from Loch Torridon—a fish of 6 lb. which was caught by a friend of mine, Ernest Tame, in March 1940.

Ernie considers that the best tackle for whiting is a three-boom paternoster, with No. 9 hooks. He usually baits his bottom hook with a cockle, the second with a strip of herring or mackerel, while the top hook holds a large mussel. They move around in large shoals and once located use of ground-bait will keep them round the tackle. The ground-bait used at Shieldaig is comprised of

mashed crabs and entrails of fish. On the south coast of England I have used a similar ground-bait with a fair amount of success.

The whiting is not a fighter. To get the best out of it for the table it should be cooked within twelve hours of being caught.

Illustration Key
1. Cockle
2. Herring
3. Mussel

**THE BEST VALUE IN FISHING BOOKS
WHY PAY MORE?**